Mortimer's Math

Patterns

Karen Bryant-Mole

Gareth Stevens Publishing
MILWAUKEE

Mortimer's Math

For a free color catalog describing Gareth Stevens' list of high-quality books and multimedia
programs, call 1-800-542-2595 (USA) or 1-800-461-9120 (Canada).
Gareth Stevens Publishing's Fax: (414) 225-0377.

Library of Congress Cataloging-in-Publication Data available upon request from publisher.
Fax: (414) 225-0377 for the attention of the Publishing Records Department.

ISBN 0-8368-2618-3

This North American edition first published in 2000 by
Gareth Stevens Publishing
1555 North RiverCenter Drive, Suite 201
Milwaukee, WI 53212 USA

This edition © 2000 by Gareth Stevens, Inc. Original © BryantMole Books, 1999. First published in 1999
by Evans Brothers Limited, 2A Portman Mansions, Chiltern Street, London W1M 1LE, United Kingdom.
Additional end matter © 2000 by Gareth Stevens, Inc.

Created by Karen Bryant-Mole
Photographs by Zul Mukhida
Designed by Jean Wheeler
Teddy bear by Merrythought Ltd.

Printed in the United States of America

1 2 3 4 5 6 7 8 9 04 03 02 01 00

contents

patterns

Mortimer the bear has some colorful building blocks. He has arranged them in a pattern.

My pattern is:
red, blue,
red, blue,
red, blue,
red, blue.

Mortimer has made another pattern using the same colors. Instead of using building blocks, he has used clothespins!

You can make patterns with almost anything.

Mortimer has made a pattern using toys.

Mortimer's pattern is:
boat, whale,
boat, whale,
boat, whale.

Look at the toys
I have used.

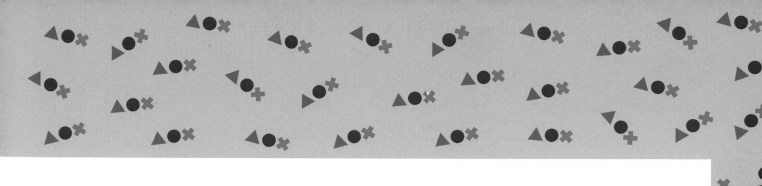

Here is another pattern that uses toys.

Can you name the pattern?

shapes

Mortimer has made a pattern with shapes.

I have used blocks that are two different shapes.

Mortimer used one shape and then the other. He repeated this over and over.

Here are some more shape patterns.
Each pattern is made up of two different shapes.

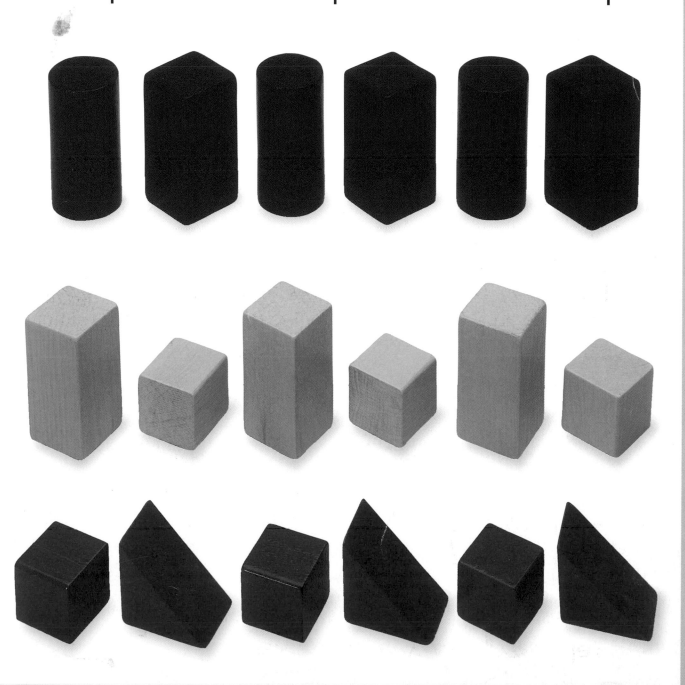

This pattern is a little more difficult.

I have used socks to make this pattern.

Mortimer's pattern is:
blue, blue, pink, pink,
blue, blue, pink, pink.

Here are some more patterns that are like the sock pattern.

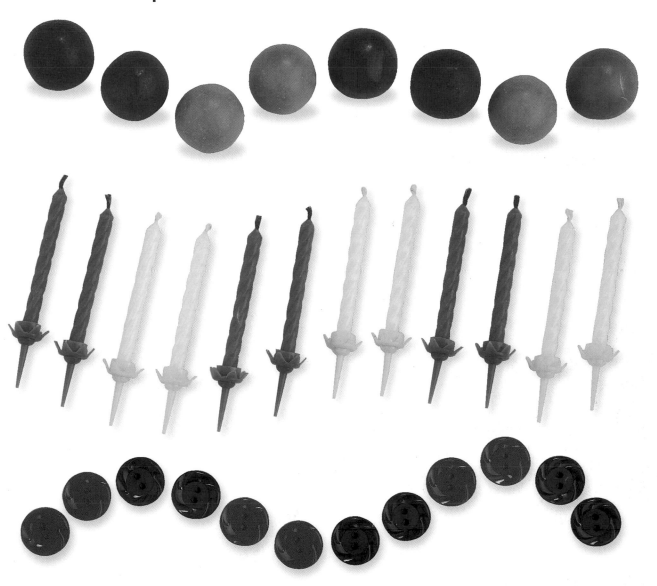

These patterns also have two of one color and then two of a different color.

size

Mortimer's toy elephants are all the same color and all the same shape.

Can you see how I made my pattern?

Mortimer's pattern has to do with size.

His pattern is:
big, small,
big, small,
big, small.

Mortimer has used lots of ducks to make another pattern that has to do with size.

Which duck should I choose next?

Think carefully about this pattern.
It might help if you say the sizes out loud.

Mortimer's pattern is:
big, small, small,
big, small, small.
So the big duck had to go next.

All these patterns have been made with different sizes. Say the sizes out loud.

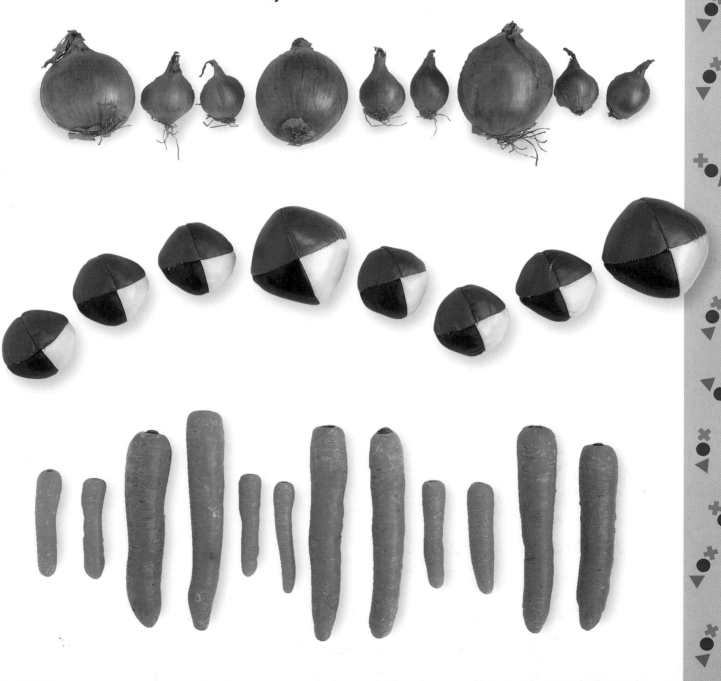

three colors

This pattern uses three different colors.

Mortimer's pattern is:
pink, blue, green,
pink, blue, green,
pink, blue, green.

Mortimer is making a necklace with spools.
He just put on the green spool.
He wants to add one
more spool.

Which color
do you think I
should choose?

Mortimer has finished his necklace.
He chose the red spool.

The pattern
I used was:
red, blue, green,
red, blue, green,
red, blue, green.

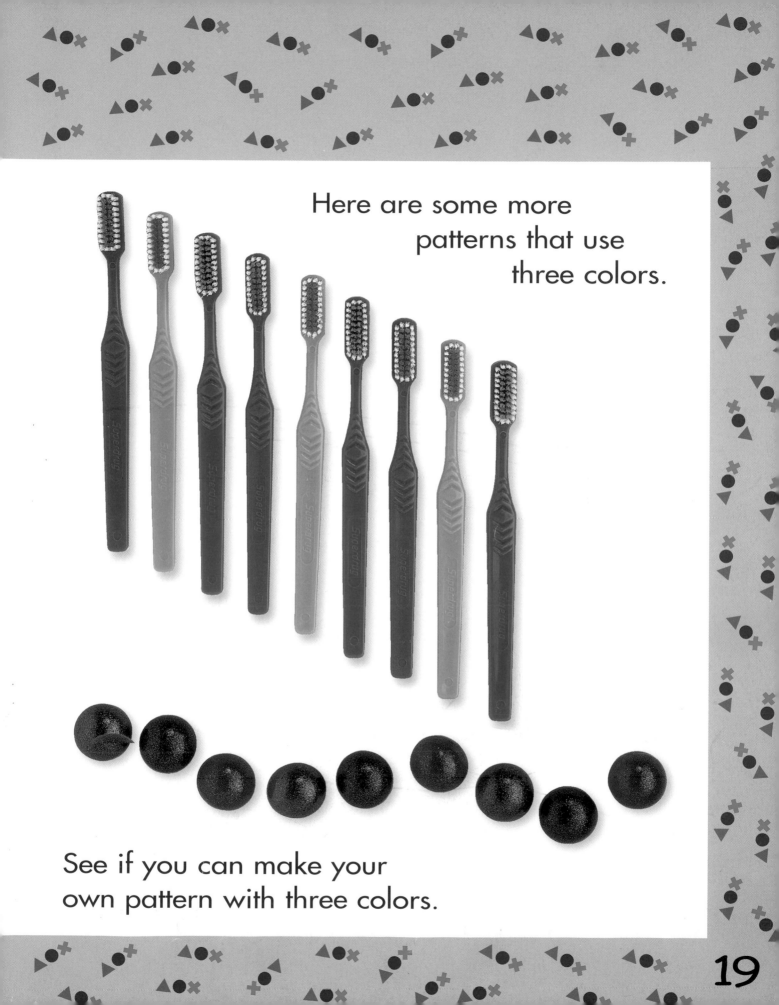

Here are some more
patterns that use
three colors.

See if you can make your
own pattern with three colors.

fruit patterns

Mortimer made this pattern with oranges and bananas!

Say the names of the fruits out loud.

This pattern is:
orange, orange, banana,
orange, orange, banana,
orange, orange, banana.

Mortimer is using plums, grapes, and strawberries to make this pattern.

What should I put next to the strawberry?

This is a tricky pattern. Don't forget! Say the names of the fruits out loud.

Mortimer's pattern is:

plum, grape, grape, strawberry,
plum, grape, grape, strawberry,
plum, grape, grape, strawberry.

Here is a long, wiggly
pattern made from fruit.
See if you can name the pattern.

glossary/index

videos

Get Ready for Math. Step Ahead series. (Western Publishing Co.)

Patterns. (The Kentucky Network)

Patterns. (United Learning, Inc.)